Original title:
The Thicket's Thoughts

Copyright © 2025 Creative Arts Management OÜ
All rights reserved.

Author: Charles Whitfield
ISBN HARDBACK: 978-1-80567-303-3
ISBN PAPERBACK: 978-1-80567-602-7

Textures of Nature's Whispers

Beneath the leaves, a squirrel grins,
With acorns piled, it's where he spins.
A leaf slips down, it tickles toes,
And laughter blooms where the wild grass grows.

A snail in armor, slow and grand,
Claims every raindrop, his tiny land.
The daisies giggle, their heads a-bob,
As bees play tag, it's quite the job.

Breezes Carrying Forgotten Tunes

An owl hoots jazz in a croaky beat,
While branches sway to the grove's own heat.
Crickets are drummers with legs so long,
Composing serenades to the night's sweet song.

A breeze blows laughter through rustled ferns,
As nature jives, the whole world turns.
The moon chuckles, hanging like a lamp,
While shadows dance, all cozy and cramped.

A Labyrinth of Living Thoughts

In tangled roots, a spider schemes,
Weaving dreams with silken beams.
A hedgehog sneezes, oh what a sight!
With tiny snorts, he takes to flight.

Mossy paths, a riddle's embrace,
Whispers giggle, revealing their grace.
The wind tells jokes, a gentle tease,
While flowers nod with the greatest ease.

Dreams Cradled in the Undergrowth

A toad croaks tales of yesteryear,
To passing frogs who stop to cheer.
Bright mushrooms dance in a dainty line,
While ants march on, quite drunk on wine.

Beneath the bramble, whispers of fun,
As ladybugs swap tales of the sun.
The shadows giggle, a muffled sound,
In the cozy nook where dreams abound.

Echoes of Hidden Paths

In shadows where whispers play,
Squirrels trade tales of the day.
Beneath the pines, a secret fall,
A croaking frog joins in the call.

Matters of nuts and seeds discussed,
Each acorn claims, 'In me, you trust!'
With giggles and twirls, they scurry about,
Nature's jesters, never in doubt.

Rustling leaves sing songs of cheer,
A woodpecker drums, 'I'm over here!'
Bumblebees buzz to their own little beat,
While ants line dance with tiny feet.

In this jolly wood, nothing's amiss,
Even the fox thinks he's a bliss.
With all these creatures, laughter unfolds,
In hidden paths, the fun never grows old.

Dreaming Underleaf

Beneath the branches, shadows twirl,
A dandelion's dream makes a swirl.
Grasshoppers croon their rhythmic tune,
While ladybugs plot 'neath the moon.

A snail slowly joins the laurel parade,
With all his shell, he's unafraid.
'What's on the menu?' asks a wise old toad,
'Just some sweet moss!' - Nature's abode.

Tickling breezes make everyone laugh,
As twigs tell stories, they cut paths in half.
Falling leaves dance with unabashed flair,
Each gust of wind, a funny affair.

In the shade, chuckles and snickers abound,
Each small creature knows they're renowned.
For dreams spark joy in the leafy embrace,
A hidden world, a bizarre, funny place.

Reflections of the Foliage

Under the green, where quirks intertwine,
A bear caught singing? Well, that's just fine!
The raccoons gossip, 'Did you see his dance?'
While the owl hoots, giving wisdom a chance.

'Who stole my berries?' yells the fuming sprite,
While mushrooms giggle at the silly sight.
Bunny rabbits play hopscotch on the grass,
Not caring at all if they trip or pass.

Dandelions plot with daffodils bold,
Wagering on who can grow fastest, uncontrolled.
Butterflies flutter, whispers in the breeze,
'Have you heard the news? The hedgehog just sneezed!'

In this leafy realm, laughter never slips,
As nature's revelers take joyful trips.
With every rustle, a chuckle's induced,
In foliage's embrace, hilarity's produced.

The Silent Counsel of Branches

The wise old maple offers advice,
On how to avoid that pesky mice.
While tulips giggle, with petals aglow,
'What's the secret to being so slow?'

Under the oak, the chatter's intense,
Debating the merits of camouflage dense.
A chipmunk insists he out ran the breeze,
While a crow caws, 'Oh please, just freeze!'

Among the sycamores, secrets they spread,
Of bounty and folly, of poppy seed bread.
Laughter echoes, as vines intertwine,
Creating a tapestry, quite divine.

Politeness rules in shadows so bold,
Where laughter from branches makes legends unfold.
Every rustle's a tale, comedic delight,
In a world of whispers, the moon shines bright.

Soft Convictions in the Moss

In the softest moss they plot,
A secret club, but they forgot.
The squirrels wear tiny ties,
While the toadstools wink their eyes.

Mushrooms dance, oh what a sight,
Mice debate on left or right.
A snail brings cupcakes, round and sweet,
While ants tap-dance on little feet.

Musings Amidst the Briars

In briars thick, a hedgehog sighs,
Contemplating life beneath the skies.
"Why can't I prance like those with wings?"
Yet wiggles cheer, as laughter sings.

A rabbit hops and claims the throne,
King of carrots, all alone.
With every bite, he grins so wide,
"I rule this patch, can't let it slide!"

Dreams Weaved in Canopies

Underneath the leafy veil,
Squirrels spin the grandest tale.
With acorns as their treasure map,
They dream of cheese, a splendid lap.

A wise old owl hoots a joke,
While sloths chill, and often poke.
The fireflies flash, they can't resist,
A dance-off game, they can't be missed.

Meditations by Dappled Light

In dappled light, the frogs convene,
To meditate on what they mean.
"Jumping high should be our creed!"
Said one, quite wise, and took the lead.

A raccoon giggles, hiding bright,
While shadows play with pure delight.
"Let's have a feast! Bring all your friends!"
And laughter echoes, never ends.

Luminescence Among the Shadows

In the dark, a squirrel pranced,
Chasing shadows, it really danced.
A twinkle glowed from a firefly,
"Wish I could catch you!" he did sigh.

A wise owl gave a knowing hoot,
"That glow's too quick for your little pursuit!"
The squirrel shrugged, said with a grin,
"In the dark, I still have my win!"

The Glistening of Twilit Pact

Under the moon, the raccoons convene,
With bandit masks, they plan their scene.
Stealing sweets from picnic baskets,
They munch and laugh, such happy caskets.

A hedgehog rolled in a nearby patch,
"Are you guys planning a midnight snatch?"
"Of course not!" declared the raccoon chief,
"We're just here for snacks, it's quite brief!"

Tales Evoked by Foliate Shadows

In the bushes, a cricket sings,
Of wild adventures and funny flings.
A turtle chuckled, quite out of breath,
"I've heard tales much better than death!"

The rabbit piped in with a twitching nose,
"You're still too slow, let's see who blows!"
They raced through leaves, the end was near,
But they just tumbled, rolling in cheer!"

A Canvas of Nature's Reflections

A painted frog on a lily pad,
Thought he was chic, he looked quite mad.
With each jump, he splashed colors about,
"I'm an art exhibit!" he did shout!

Nearby, a beetle, in shiny black,
Said, "Your art? It's just a quack!"
But with a wink and a whimsical spin,
The frog laughed loud, let the fun begin!"

The Lattice of Leafy Dreams

In a nest of twisted vines,
A squirrel swears he's sipping wines.
He tells a tale of leafy quests,
While raccoons ponder their fashion tests.

The rabbit claims he found a shoe,
Worn by a hedgehog—true, it's blue!
They dance around, quite merry indeed,
As bugs form bands, their music freed.

A chipmunk hosts a picnic feast,
With acorn pie—a nutty beast!
The ants bring plankton, slim and sweet,
While crickets tap their tiny feet.

So gather 'round this leafy stage,
For every critter plays a page.
With laughter loud and smiles so wide,
In dreams of leaves, they all abide.

Sounds of the Subterranean

Deep below where shadows play,
A mole debates in a funny way.
He claims his tunnel is a maze,
While worms roll eyes in an earthy daze.

With echoes bouncing off the walls,
Each croak and burp breaks echo halls.
The bats have formed a gossip crew,
Trading secrets, nearly flew!

A snail joins in on the ruckus,
Dragging behind a tiny focus.
He speaks in rhymes so slow and grand,
While insects chuckle, close at hand.

And in this realm of dirt and stone,
They find a joy that feels like home.
So listen close, beneath your feet,
For laughter's warmth in underground heat!

The Fabric of Ferny Fancies

Among the fronds, a fabric spins,
With woven tales of unlikely wins.
A chameleon wears stripes of plaid,
While ladybugs giggle at what he had.

The ferns hold rallies, oh so green,
With whispers of fashion like you've never seen.
They decide to flutter, spin, and sway,
While snails film it all—what a wild play!

And then a butterfly takes a bow,
She's tangled up in ferns somehow.
With patterns bright and colors bold,
She flutters tales from times of old.

In this mantled weave of dreams,
Where silliness flows in calming streams,
Each stitch of laughter knits them tight,
In the fabric of fancies, pure delight.

Resonance of the Rustling

When leaves begin their silly dance,
The critters gather, a merry prance.
A fox in sneakers leads the way,
While owls hoot tunes, they sing and sway.

With squirrels racing up the boughs,
Debating loudly—who knows how?
The wind chimes in with a giggly breeze,
As bees do cartwheels among the trees.

And there's a lizard, bold and spry,
Attempting jokes and aiming high.
His punchlines land like rocks in streams,
Making mischief in youthful dreams.

So join the chorus of rustling fun,
Where laughter echoes—a joyful run.
Amidst the branches, joy takes flight,
In the shade where silliness ignites.

Strategies of the Swaying Grass

Grass blades gossip with the breeze,
Whispering secrets with such ease.
They joke about the passing bees,
And dance like it's a grand reprise.

When raindrops come, they stage a show,
Splashing around, putting on a glow.
Each droplet a laugh, a giggle, a flow,
As puddles form, their fun starts to grow.

The sun breaks out, they strike a pose,
Basking in sunlight, striking their prose.
With each gust, they wiggle their toes,
In nature's theater, who really knows?

In a world where each blade has flair,
They hold court, like they don't have a care.
Even the wind can't help but stare,
At how they sway, without a single square.

Harmonies of the Hidden Life

In the soil, the critters sing,
Worms and bugs do their own thing.
A chorus that makes the roots swing,
While ants march in, a bustling ring.

Beetles boast of shiny shells,
Telling tales that no one tells.
In their minds, they weave great spells,
A world where every creature dwells.

A snail winks and takes its time,
With stories that are truly sublime.
Each little journey—a nursery rhyme,
In this hidden world, life's in its prime.

From sprouts to fungi, all unite,
In a hilariously chaotic sight.
Life below is a pure delight,
A symphony in the soft twilight.

Journeys Beneath the Bark

Underneath the bark, a maze,
Critters plot and navigate in a haze.
Squirrels play hide and seek, in a daze,
While fungi laugh in their cozy bays.

The woodpecker thinks it's a band,
Tapping out rhythms, oh so grand.
Joining the fun, a beetle, unplanned,
Leads a parade through this wonderland.

Vines hang low, inviting a chat,
With a lazy lizard, sprawled out flat.
Their laughter echoes, how about that?
In this world, no room for a spat.

As twilight falls, the whispers play,
Keeping secrets of the day.
In their realm, where mischief holds sway,
Laughter blooms, come what may.

Tangles of Time in the Green

Time gets tangled in emerald leaves,
Where every rustle is a story that weaves.
Chirping crickets join in with ease,
Turning the dusk into a symphony that cleaves.

A squirrel with a nut, thinks he's the king,
Hoarding treasures like it's a favorite fling.
With a leap and a bound, he makes spring,
While robins chirp and joyfully cling.

As shadows stretch, the owls begin to plot,
Hooting and howling, giving it a shot.
In their wise antics, we find a lot,
Wise cracks and jokes—it's hilariously hot.

So in this haven, laughter is fine,
In tangled tales where we intertwine.
Every moment, a chance to shine,
In the green arena of the divine.

Timid Voices in the Brush

A squirrel shouts, "I lost my nuts!"
But all that's found are sleepy sluts.
The rabbits giggle, hiding away,
As feisty weeds start to sway.

A crow remarks, quite out of turn,
"The sun's too hot, it's making me burn!"
Yet on he sits, with wings all wide,
Wishing for shade, though he won't hide.

The hedgehogs mutter in secret chats,
Debating styles of different hats.
One wants spikes, the other a bow,
They'd steal the show, if only they'd grow!

A fox walks by, all suave and sleek,
But trips on roots, and lands with a squeak.
The laughter echoes, a merry sound,
In every bush where jokes abound.

Fluttering Thoughts in the Breeze

A butterfly flutters, pondering deft,
"Who needs a map? I'm surely blessed!"
But as it twists, with colors grand,
It finds itself in a daisy's hand.

A ladybug claims she's fashion's queen,
Voicing dreams of a life serene.
Yet when the rain starts pouring down,
She complains of mud, and pulls a frown.

Grasshoppers leap, with boisterous pride,
While ants march on, quite side by side.
"We're the real athletes of this place,"
Said one, bringing fit in a happy race.

The wind makes fun of buzzing bees,
"You're all just here to steal my breeze!"
They bark back, in a flurry and buzz,
For they know, without them, there's no fuzz.

Tangled Whispers of the Earth

In tangled roots, a worm did squirm,
"This shade feels nice, oh what a term!"
But then a kid with muddy feet,
Steps on his head—now that's no treat.

A snail's slow gossip floats through the muck,
"Did you hear? That frog nearly got plucked!"
But Mr. Frog hops with a grin,
"I'm too bouncy — let the fun begin!"

Twigs gossiping like old-time bats,
"Who knew here we'd become chitchat cats?"
While mushrooms chime in, so bold and spry,
"Don't forget we thrive, but never fly!"

The earthworms laugh with wiggly glee,
"Stay hidden, kids, it's the best way to be!"
While leaves crack jokes above in the air,
As the roots below dance with a flair.

The Mind of the Forest Floor

Mushrooms ponder the meaning of shade,
"Is it our hats, or are we just made?"
They laugh and stack, a towering heap,
Until a deer swoops by, making them weep.

Nearby, a chipmunk recounts a thrill,
"I found a stash, it's my biggest bill!"
But tree bark chuckles, wise and old,
"Just wait, my friend, till winter is cold!"

Leaves ruffle softly, sharing a tune,
"Did you see that squirrel? He danced like a loon!"
There's joy in the shadows and fun in the dark,
Where giggles abound and experiences spark.

Crisp pine needles tickle the feet,
While critters conspire for a snack that's sweet.
With every cheer and uproarious jest,
The forest floor knows how to jest best!

Emotions Buried Deep in Soil

Worms play poker with the roots,
They giggle as they wiggle suits.
Rabbits gossip, tails in a flurry,
While moles dig deep, but don't you worry.

A squirrel jokes of acorn debts,
While trees roll their bark and place their bets.
Grass blades whisper of silly dreams,
Where flowers dance in sunlight's beams.

Yet down below in the dirt's embrace,
The secrets swirl in a lively race.
Laughter rings from the bugs who chirp,
Nature's punchlines packaged in a burp!

So every root, every leaf, every sprout,
Holds a joke that's waiting to shout.
When you dig in, don't be surprised,
To find the humor that nature disguised.

Whimsical Whiskers of Nature

A fox with glasses, reading a book,
Pondering life with a thoughtful look.
Critters gather for a comedy night,
Where shadows dance and laughter takes flight.

The owl shares wisdom, but slips on a branch,
While fireflies twinkle in a bright, flashy dance.
Bees tell tales of nectar heists,
Buzzing around with their sweet, sticky fests.

A hedgehog, dressed as a fashionista,
Struts down the path with a flair like a diva.
The daisies clap in a flowered cheer,
For nature's runway is finally here!

In this woodland show, glee's a must,
As bark beetles boogie, zesting up the dust.
Whiskers of woods tickling the air,
Each chuckle resounds in this funny affair.

Verses from the Veins of Trees

A tree with a joke tucked deep in its bark,
Tells it to owls that hoot after dark.
They cackle and caw, 'till branches do shake,
While saplings giggle, their roots start to quake!

Leaves stretch and flutter, practicing lines,
As a breeze drifts by, spinning tales in designs.
The woodpecker drums on a trunk with flair,
Dropping punchlines, trees shake with despair.

Nutty squirrels stage a play in the sun,
Where acorns are actors, oh what a fun!
The wildflowers bloom, as the curtains arise,
In this forest theater, laughter defies!

So climb up a branch, if you're curious too,
Find the humor in nature and join in the view.
For every ring that tells time's gentle tease,
Whispers of chuckles flow down through the trees.

Inquiries Amidst the Shrubs

Hey there, do bushes really talk?
Or is it just critters taking a walk?
A raccoon asks, his head tilted with glee,
"Why don't flowers ever charge a fee?"

The twigs snap back with a rustling jest,
"Because you'd be broke, and that's for the best!"
The thorns interject with a prickly tease,
"Stop asking, our jokes are harder to please!"

A lizard lounges, sunbathing with pride,
"I'd tell you a tale, but I've not the drive!"
And nearby a snail says, with patience quite grand,
"Slow down my friends, let chaos expand!"

In this dappled maze where whimsy prevails,
Questions fly freely, carried by gales.
Nature's banter spins sweet melodies,
Every shrub is a comedian, just wait and see!

The Colors of the Hidden Trail

In woods where whispers play,
The squirrels paint their day.
A purple twig, a yellow leaf,
They giggle, oh so brief.

A green-eyed frog hops high,
Wearing spots like a tie.
He croaks out jokes galore,
And leaves us wanting more.

Beneath the brush, the flowers grin,
Their petals bright, a wild spin.
The daisies sway to the beat,
While ants march in retreat.

In daylight's dance, the colors clash,
As butterflies flash in a dash.
The hues all laugh and shout,
What a riot, without a doubt!

Dance of the Flickering Fauna

Fireflies swing with a twirl,
Their light, a glowing whirl.
With a wink and a twist,
They vanish in the mist.

A raccoon steals the scene,
With a mask that's quite serene.
He juggles nuts with flair,
While critters stop and stare.

A rabbit leaps to the tune,
Underneath the watchful moon.
His ears bounce like balloons,
While owls chuckle in swoons.

As dusk falls with a sigh,
The forest waves goodbye.
In dreams, the animals prance,
Forever in their dance!

Silent Reveries of the Moss

A patch of moss feels grand,
Like a carpet, soft and bland.
It dreams of woodland tales,
Where gossip never fails.

Beneath the shade, the fungi sprout,
Whispering secrets, no doubt.
They chuckle with delight,
In shadows, out of sight.

A slug slides by with grace,
Leaving trails, its own trace.
He boasts of epic quests,
While snails take little rests.

In quiet, mossy beds do lie,
The humor, never shy.
With smiles hidden and stirred,
Their whispers barely heard!

Sagas from the Secreted Glen

In glens where secrets bloom,
A gopher spins tales of doom.
He narrates with a squeak,
About the fox's sneak.

A badger strolls with pride,
Wearing stripes that can't hide.
He tells of snowy nights,
Where he outsmarted fights.

The chatter from the ferns so bright,
As rabbits tale the night.
Their laughter brings delight,
Beneath starlit sight.

As twilight blushes anew,
The stories swell and grew.
In the glen, the whimsy flows,
Where every tale truly glows!

Nature's Silent Confessions

The squirrels plot with acorn spies,
While owls roll their big round eyes.
They chuckle at humans quite bewildered,
As nature's secrets stay well-rounded.

The flowers gossip, petals a-flutter,
Whispering tales while bees just mutter.
Rabbits hop in fashionable ease,
Wearing their coats, just like a tease.

A turtle grins, though slow in pace,
He's got all the time in this race.
As sunbeams dance on the leaves so green,
They share smirks only they have seen.

A breeze comes through, with laughter loud,
Tickling the grasses, making them proud.
In nature's realm, jesters abound,
In every nook, a giggle is found.

Murmurs of the Forest Floor

The mushrooms chat in colors bright,
Teasing bugs that skip in flight.
A chipmunk stands, tail up high,
As if to say, "No need to be shy!"

Leaves rustle softly, like whispers sweet,
Making up jokes with each little beat.
A snail slinks in, taking his time,
Claiming the path as his grand climb.

A pinecone drops, a prankster's throw,
Landing gently on a frog below.
That frog jumps high with quite a splash,
While laughter's echo makes quite the bash.

In shadows deep, a hedgehog snorts,
While finding the snacks of forest courts.
Each giggle shared among the trees,
Turns nature's stage into a tease.

Meditations in the Midst of Green

A bumblebee dreams of endless flight,
While daydreaming of a treat so right.
Fragrant flowers sway in sync,
As if they know more than we think.

The grasshoppers jump with glee,
Playing tag in harmony.
"Catch me if you can!" they shout,
As ants march on, without a doubt.

A wise old owl with quirky glances,
Chimes in on their silly dances.
He rolls his eyes at all the fuss,
While pondering which tree to trust.

The sun winks down, casting its light,
As critters gather, their hearts so bright.
In laughter's echo, they all proclaim,
Nature's joy is out to gain!

Conversations with the Wind

The wind zips through, with tales to tell,
Spinning stories, casting a spell.
It tugs at leaves, a playful tease,
While whistling tunes with utter ease.

The grasses wave, like hands in cheer,
Waving hello, with nary a fear.
The flowers nod, swaying in line,
They chuckle softly, "Oh, we're fine!"

A crow caws loud, in a husky tone,
Witty banter, he calls his own.
As squirrels giggle, tails in a knot,
In this grand chatter, joy is caught.

The wind carries on, with laughter fair,
Fluttering joy is everywhere.
In nature's breath, humor does weave,
A merry dance, for all who believe.

Folded Pages of the Forest

In leafy realms where whispers play,
Squirrels plot their heist today.
Beneath the boughs, a debate ensues,
Who stole the snacks? The raccoon, or the moose?

Mushrooms giggle as they bloom,
Sharing secrets amidst the gloom.
A turtle dances, slow yet spry,
While crickets roll their eyes nearby.

Branches sway with mischievous cheer,
Echoing laughter, oh so clear.
Even the stones chuckle sometimes,
Rolling their eyes at the silly climbs.

Nature's stage of playful delight,
Critters' antics, oh what a sight!
Each folded page tells a tale anew,
In this lively forest full of view.

The Quiet Companions of the Thicket

Beneath the shrubs, a secret crew,
Bunnies giggle at clouds askew.
A wise old owl with glasses perched,
Sips his tea, while squirrels are searched.

Bees play tag, buzzing with glee,
While ladybugs stake out the plea.
A hedgehog hums a serenade,
As flowers bloom, their colors parade.

Mice with maps explore the nooks,
Writing stories in tiny books.
Frogs sing opera in dulcet tones,
While roots rhyme softly, in hushed drone.

Twilight brings tales of comical feats,
Under the moon, the laughter repeats.
With every rustle and shuffle in sight,
Quiet companions, the essence of light.

Landscapes of Untamed Fantasies

A canvas sprawls of green and brown,
Where critters laugh and none wear a frown.
A fox in a hat, oh what style!
Bears exchanging jokes, they sit for a while.

In the creek, fish laugh at the ducks,
While turtles tell tales of nifty luck.
A chameleon appears just for fun,
Changing colors, 'Watch me run!'

Wind joins in with a playful hum,
As dandelions join the fun.
Each pathway's a giggle, each tree a grin,
In this wildland, where dreams begin.

Nature's palette, bright and bold,
Stories of mischief, never old.
In corners hidden, oh what a sight,
The fantasies flourish, day and night.

Simmering Stories of the Wild

Bamboo shakes, a puppet show,
With raccoons playing, stealing the glow.
Giraffes gossip about the clouds,
While geese squawk, gathering crowds.

A parrot tells jokes that spread like fire,
While deer dance under the moon with desire.
Vines twist and twirl in laughter's embrace,
As shadows perform with whimsical grace.

Each flicker of light's a tale untold,
Whispering secrets, both warm and cold.
Nature brews tales in simmering pots,
Mixing up giggles in tangled knots.

In the wild where stories ignite,
Every moment's a sheer delight.
With each leaf's flutter, we find our way,
In a comedy sketch of the bright and brave.

Fragments of Nature's Whimsy

A squirrel in a hat spins around,
Chasing after nuts that tumble down.
The flowers giggle, colors in play,
As bees buzz softly, stealing the day.

A rabbit with glasses reads a small book,
While ants in a line do a dance and a cook.
The trees shake with laughter, leaves in a stew,
As butterflies gossip about who likes blue.

Under the sun, the humor takes flight,
Even the mushrooms are grinning with delight.
Nature's own jesters, they put on a show,
With whispers of joy in the soft summer glow.

So come join the fun, leave your woes far behind,
In this world of mischief, a joy you shall find.
Where every small critter, in its own little way,
Keeps chuckling and frolicking day after day.

A Tapestry of Bark and Leaf

Leaves don outfits, colors so bright,
Dancing and twirling, a whimsical sight.
Bark tells stories of days gone by,
With a twist of the winds and a rustle nearby.

A raccoon in boots prances through the grass,
While snails in tuxedos take pride as they pass.
The puddles reflect a sky full of jest,
As frogs croak their jokes, never taking a rest.

Beetles play drums, a band on the run,
With ladybugs singing, oh what fun!
The essence of laughter floats high in the air,
In this enchanted realm where joy is laid bare.

So let your heart skip, come join the parade,
In this tapestry woven, where silliness played.
With leaves as our banners, and joy as our creed,
We'll dance through the forest, fulfilling a need.

Soulful Canopies

In the canopy high, a party takes flight,
With owls telling jokes into the dark night.
Raccoons juggling acorns, filling the air,
With laughter that sparkles like songs everywhere.

The trees sway their branches, a musical tune,
As fireflies twinkle, illuminating the gloom.
Crickets provide rhythm, a beat like a drum,
While hedgehogs spin tales of where they are from.

A woodpecker knocks, a comedic refrain,
As squirrels roll over, unable to feign.
Each creature enthralled in this whimsical cheer,
Nature's own theater, the stage is so near.

So come, if you dare, to this joyous display,
Where laughter and light chase the shadows away.
With soulful canopies, thick as they seem,
We weave through the night, living each dream.

The Lullaby of Unseen Creatures

In the depths of the night, where shadows do peek,
The unseen creatures play hide and seek.
A vixen sings softly, serenades clear,
While owls roll their eyes; oh dear, what a year!

Mice in their microcosm, crafting delights,
As fireflies twinkle like wonderful lights.
A fox shares a tale with a wise old toad,
Who nods with great humor, hidden down the road.

The crickets strum gently, keeping the beat,
As hedgehogs discuss their last evening's feast.
The laughter of night, a well-kept disguise,
Bringing smiles in silence, under starry skies.

So listen quite closely, there's magic in flight,
From creatures unseen, till the return of light.
With whispers and chuckles, their tales intertwine,
In a lullaby woven, oh what a divine!

Confessions of the Bark

Once a squirrel blamed me for his fall,
I just laughed and stood tall, after all.
With a grin I watched him scurry away,
His acorn stash lost, what a silly display.

I've seen bunnies in their finest attire,
Hopping around like they're on fire!
But they trip on clovers, oh what a sight,
Twisting and tumbling—no grace in their flight.

The birds chirp gossip from way up high,
About a moth who thinks he can fly.
He flits and flutters, oh what a tease,
But the wind laughs harder, "Not with such ease!"

At night I listen to owls so wise,
Debating the best way to catch their flies.
Their feathery whispers drift through the night,
While crickets join in for a musical fight.

Reveries Among the Ferns

In shady patches, where the ferns sway,
The rabbits gather to gossip and play.
With their floppy ears flapping in style,
They trade old secrets and giggle awhile.

A raccoon dropped by, wearing a mask,
In search of mischief, what a wild task!
He knocked over mushrooms, oh what a mess,
"Not me!" he exclaimed, with feigned innocence.

The slugs slide in, such slimy delight,
With tales of travels under moonlight.
They laugh at the snails, so slow and so shy,
"Just take your time, you'll get there by and by!"

With each rustle, the tales never cease,
Of feathered capers and abounding peace.
A dance of laughter in green shades so bright,
As twilight wraps them in soft, starry light.

Insights in the Gloom

In the shadows where whispers tend to creep,
A wise old toad starts his nightly leap.
He croaks out riddles, strange but profound,
Pondering life from the murky ground.

The fireflies giggle, flickering bright,
Flashing their numbers as they take flight.
"Count us if you can!" they flicker and tease,
While the old toad chuckles, "Oh please, oh please!"

Mice scurry by, holding a debate,
On cheese preferences: oh, what a fate!
"Is it cheddar or brie?" they ponder and squeak,
Meanwhile the shadows just chuckle, "So bleak!"

In this dim world, laughter echoes wide,
With critters sharing jokes they can't abide.
Each chuckle and chirp, a curious tune,
Bringing light to the secrets of the moon.

Phantoms of the Underbrush

Among the thorns where shadows do play,
Lurk phantoms of laughter, come out to sway.
A wise old fox, with a twitch of his tail,
Shares tales of the night—oh, do not derail!

"Have you seen the deer, wearing socks?" he sneers,
Chasing their friends through the dandelions' cheers.
With long-legged strides, they leap and they mock,
Dodging the owls, as they gather and flock.

The skunks, overly bold, strut around proud,
Holding their noses above the loud crowd.
"Who needs a partner?" one sneezes in jest,
While the trees just chuckle at their silly fest.

As laughter bursts forth from the underbrush,
Each critter joins in for a rollicking rush.
These phantoms of mirth, they dance and they sway,
Creeping through night, making mischief their play.

Serendipity Among the Wildflowers

In the meadow, bees do tango,
Flitting 'round like they're in stango,
Dandelions wear a crown of gold,
Whispering secrets, tales untold.

Butterflies laugh in vibrant hues,
Stomping the daisies, they've got the blues,
A ladybug winks, says, "What's the fuss?"
Twirling around like it's all for us.

Grasshoppers leap with a comic flair,
Bouncing about without a care,
"Hop on my back!" chirps a chatty ant,
Off to a picnic, so quaint and gallant.

In this riot of colors, mischief prevails,
Every petal giggles, every leaf trails,
A ruckus of joy, let laughter abound,
Nature's humor can truly astound!

The Mind of a Mossy Stone

Sitting quietly, the moss makes a throne,
"Who's got the brain?" says the wise old stone,
A snail quips, "You'll need a pot of tea,
For all these thoughts that keep haunting me!"

Frog croaks theories, leaping to reason,
"Life's just a hop, it's all in the season!"
Moss chuckles back, "That's quite the jest,
You think you're so smart, but I'm just the best!"

Raindrops gather, a blundering crew,
"Don't slip on us, or we'll splash you too!"
The stone just smiles, a stoic old sage,
"Funny how laughter makes me feel age!"

In this chatty realm where rocks find their muse,
Antics aplenty, no time to snooze,
With every giggle, wisdom is sown,
The mind of a stone is never alone!

Traces of the Unexplored

A path less traveled, oh what a tease,
"Where does it lead?" asks a rustling breeze,
Whiskers of grass tickle my feet,
Curiosity dances in summer's heat.

A squirrel debates life choices aloud,
"Do I climb high or blend with the crowd?"
Meanwhile, old oak gabs with a crow,
"Life's a surprise, let's put on a show!"

Patches of clover conspire and scheme,
Growing wild, they'll dodge the routine dream,
A raccoon pops up, "Did you see that?"
"It's just a worm!" says a chatty bat.

With whispers of wonder in every nook,
Life's a mishap, come write the book,
Through chuckles and giggles, the unknown awaits,
Treasure the silly, let joy be our fate!

Nature's Diary of Delight

In the orchard, fruit revolts with glee,
Cherries compete for the highest decree,
"Pick me first!" the apples shout loud,
As giggles form round a browsing crowd.

The wind whirls by with a tune in its heart,
Singing to leaves like a playful art,
"Catch me if you can!" taunts a spritely thorn,
While daisies chuckle at the sudden storm.

A field of corn wears a crown of curls,
"Join us!" they whisper, "Let's twirl and whirl!"
Sunflowers nod in a dance so sweet,
As dandelions tumble and skip on their feet.

Joy paints the canvas of nature's spree,
With every giggle, so wild and free,
In pages of laughter, the world gleams bright,
Nature's own diary scribes splashes of light!

Secrets Entwined in Ferns

In the ferns, whispers collide,
Secrets that critters do hide.
A squirrel, with acorns galore,
Claims it's all just a folklore.

A raccoon, with mischievous glee,
Sips from the puddle, says, "Look at me!"
His mask on his face, quite absurd,
He thinks he's the star of the world.

The ladybugs gossip in style,
Over a cup, they chit-chat and smile.
"Did you hear what the owl said?"
"No, but I'd love to, up in my bed!"

Dance of the toads, jumpy and spry,
While the grasshoppers sing in the sky.
With every croak, a laughter unfolds,
Nature's giggles, pure gold untold.

Flickers of Light Through Branches

Sunbeams play, a lighthearted dance,
A bunny hops in a blissful trance.
The shadows tease with a wiggle and sway,
While the woodpecker's jokes land wildly astray.

The deer prances, wearing a leafy crown,
Wonders if she should wear that to town.
A squirrel cracks nuts, the punchline in sight,
"What did the acorn say? You're just not my type!"

Amidst the flip of a butterfly wing,
The crickets perform, with a chorus they sing.
Each flicker of light, a giggly tease,
Nature's own jester, a flair for the breeze.

So here in the woods, bright flashes amuse,
With every chuckle, more joy to choose.
The sun sinks low, the laughter won't cease,
In this merry realm, all find their peace.

Dappled Thoughts on a Rainy Day

Pitter-patter, the raindrops tap,
A squirrel in yellow, takes a quick nap.
Leaves twist and turn, what a slippery scene,
Splash on the puddles, we are kings and queens.

The worms, in their coats, dance in the muck,
Chasing each other, oh, what good luck!
"Why do we wiggle?" one asks with glee,
"Because it's the only way we can be free!"

The frogs, in a choir, croak their delight,
Turning to stage, they're ready tonight.
"With a splash and a croon, we'll steal the show,
Let the rain be our audience, we'll steal the glow!"

As puddles collect, tiny boats set sail,
Imaginations soar; oh, we will prevail.
For rainy days bring fun, laughter galore,
In dappled thoughts, there's always much more.

Mindscapes of the Wild

In the wild, where oddities roam,
A fox dons a beret, claiming it's home.
Giggling trees lend their roots for a scene,
As they wave their branches, all kinds of green.

An owl on a branch makes a starry decree,
"Who's hunting here? It's definitely me!"
With a wink and a hoot, creativity flows,
In this realm of wonders, anything goes.

Mice stage a circus, a sight to behold,
Juggling seeds, a story retold.
And the butterflies flutter in poncho-shaped flair,
Dancing through fables spun from thin air.

So venture with glee through this whimsical land,
Where mindscapes of wild weave a fanciful strand.
Laughter and whimsy, a tune for the bold,
In nature's embrace, stories unfold.

Chronicles of the Shaded Grove

In the grove, the squirrels scheme,
Plotting mischief, a nutty dream.
A frog debates with a honking goose,
Who's the true king of this leafy noose?

A raccoon dons his finest hat,
Sipping dewdrops, he thinks he's fat.
The owls gossip from their tree tops,
While off-key canaries sing karaoke flops.

Beneath the boughs a rabbit hops,
Juggling acorns, the laughter pops.
Each leaf whispers a giggly tune,
As shadows dance beneath the moon.

Join the jests, come and see,
Nature's theater, wild and free.
With every chuckle, we'll roam and play,
In our shaded wonderland today!

Lonesome Lanterns in the Underbrush

A glow-worm sighs in the thick of night,
Lonely lantern, what a silly sight!
A firefly winks like a flirty star,
Saying, 'Come dance, I've traveled far!'

A hedgehog complains of a thorny mess,
While a curious owl just likes to guess.
'What's for dinner?' the stoat inquires,
The hedgehog shrugs, 'I prefer fires!'

The raccoon strums a twiggy guitar,
While the crickets chirp, not up to par.
Together they croon, oh what a cheer,
As foxes howl, 'Turn it up dear!'

In the underbrush, the fun persists,
With each blink and wink, no chance to miss.
Join the jamboree till the break of dawn,
And laugh with friends from dusk till morn!

Wilderness of Whispering Dreams

In the woods where giggles glide,
A sloth competes in a snore-off ride.
It's a heavyweight bout of snoozing grace,
With the chipmunk ready to join the race!

A grumpy badger throws a fit,
Over stolen snacks and a lost knit.
A playful fox tosses in a quip,
'Next time, let's all just share a chip!'

The deer play tag in glittering light,
As the shadowy vines dance left and right.
A bear complains, 'Where's my lunch?'
Everyone giggles at the awkward bunch!

So dream with us in this wild space,
Where funny tales leave a silly trace.
The whispers of nature, full of glee,
Join us in laughter, and feel so free!

The Spectrum of Sunlit Thoughts

In sunlit beams, the notions play,
A butterfly lands, brightening the day.
Bumblebees buzz with comedic glee,
'Join our pollinating jamboree!'

The hedgehogs roll, all prickles and fight,
In a game of tag, neither is bright.
They tumble and giggle, causing a scene,
While nearby, a lizard looks quite serene.

The trees discuss secrets, a rustling chat,
Regaling tales of a prowling cat.
'Last I saw him, he chased his own tail!'
Every leaf chuckles, 'Your humor can't fail!'

In this radiant realm, joy takes flight,
With every sunbeam, a laugh feels right.
Let's bask in the glow of our silly fate,
And dance with the shadows, let's celebrate!

Whispers of the Wild

In the hush of the woods, I heard a hare,
Telling jokes to a fox with an unruly hair.
The squirrel chimed in with a nutty pun,
While the owl rolled its eyes, 'Oh, this is fun!'

A raccoon peeked out, with a grin so wide,
'You think you can dance? Come on, take a ride!'
They twirled 'round the trees in an acorn spree,
Laughing so hard, they'd wake the old bee.

But then thunder crashed, with lightning's bright flash,
The party dispersed in a mighty dash.
The hare winked and said, with a bouncy hop,
'Next time, my friends, we'll just dance on the top!'

So the forest rejoiced in laughter and cheer,
While planning a bash under full moon's sheer.
With whispers of fun in the tall oak's shade,
Their woodland jamboree was happily made.

Shadows Beneath the Canopy

In the depths of the grove, shadows began,
A turtle declared, 'I've got a great plan!'
He called for some mice, a party to throw,
They bounced on mushrooms, and away they did go!

A chipmunk then shouted, 'Let's turn back time!'
With acorns as tokens and sap for the rhyme.
They fashioned a stage made of twigs and leaves,
To showcase their talents, and nobody leaves!

The beetles were drummers, they played on the ground,
While crickets provided a chirpy sound.
The fireflies lit up the show with their glow,
Even the grumpy old badger said, 'Whoa!'

But just as they grooved beneath the bright moon,
Along came a raccoon, shouting, 'Not so soon!'
'Your rhythm's all wrong, the steps are a mess!'
Yet they laughed till they cried, and who could care less?

Murmurs from the Undergrowth

In the depths of the grass, whispers took flight,
A snail made a pun, and it felt so right.
The toad said, 'Please, what a slippery sport!'
While a ladybug rolled, laughing hard, 'Oh, a court!'

The bugs held a meeting beneath the tall fern,
'Talk of the weather, or gossip—we learn!'
The ants brought their stories; they never were sly,
'You should see what we do when the humans walk by!'

Amidst all the laughter, a shadow did loom,
A curious cat, thinking this was a room.
She pounced for the fun, but slipped on a leaf,
And the whispers erupted in fits of disbelief!

Then a wise old tree said, 'Let's welcome her in,
Join our wild party, we all want to spin!'
And so, amidst giggles and a curious pout,
The cat learned the ways of the buzzing folk's rout.

Secrets in the Green

In a patch of bright clover, secrets did bloom,
A worm wiggled by, shouting, 'Make room!'
'I've got a story about a lost shoe,'
'And the frog who thought he could master a brew!'

With laughter a-bubbling, the daisies chimed in,
'Oh please, do tell, we all love a win!'
A butterfly danced, wings shimmering bright,
'You think you're the best? It's a hilarious sight!'

While the mushrooms held court, all eager to hear,
A mouse called out, 'I just saw a deer!'
With wiggles and giggles, they plotted a quest,
To find out the truth and put gossip to rest.

But amidst all the fun, the sun dipped low,
'Wrap it up soon, friends, the moon's here for show!'
So they promised to share more, bright secrets untold,
In the nighttime's embrace, where their laughter would unfold.

Shadows of Forgotten Twigs

In the woods, twigs have tales,
They whisper jokes, send playful trails.
A branch once dressed up in a hat,
Reported a squirrel as quite a brat.

The shadows dance, they sway and tease,
Chasing bugs, they do as they please.
A leaf fell down with a merry wink,
Said, "I'm just here to make you think!"

A rabbit hopped with a cheeky grin,
Claiming he knew where the best grass had been.
The trees chuckled at his boastful claim,
As the wind echoed back, "Just join the game!"

And so beneath the sky so blue,
Life's a jest in this leafy view.
Twigs and leaves, in merry play,
Bring laughter forth from dawn till day.

Riddles Beneath the Canopy

What falls but never gets hurt?
A raindrop joked as it hit the dirt.
A tree chuckled, "I've seen it all,
Like squirrel acrobatics and a feather fall!"

The shadows giggle, holding tight,
Secrets told in the dead of night.
A riddle here, a punchline there,
The forest laughs without a care.

The owls hoot riddles, wise yet sly,
"Why don't trees use Facebook? Oh my!"
The answers flutter on autumn's breeze,
As pine needles chuckle with such ease.

With every rustle, a new jest spun,
In the canopy where the giggles run.
Riddles bloom like flowers in spring,
In this playful realm where the woods just sing.

Echoes of the Woodland

In the woodland, echoes call,
Of mischief merry, big and small.
A chipmunk squeaked, "Who lost the race?"
While a fox just rolled, a real ace.

Branches creaked with laughter fit,
As the mushrooms join in to sit.
"Why did the pine tree lose its seat?"
"Because it couldn't stand up to the beet!"

The echoes bounce off laughter's walls,
Where even the shadow playfully sprawls.
"Got any cheese for this riddle pace?"
"Only if you bring a dance to the place!"

So gather 'round, and let's all cheer,
For the woodland's humor, sincere and clear.
In the echoes, every friend finds glee,
In this forest of joy, wild and free.

Dreams Woven in Vines

Vines weave tales of twilight fun,
With every twist, a new joy spun.
"Why do we climb?" asked a brave young sprout,
"Because up high, you can always shout!"

A clump of moss grinned, full of cheer,
"Nothing's dream-like as being here!"
"Just don't trip on that creeping vine,
For it might just want a sip of your wine!"

The leaves rustle, with whispers bold,
Stories of snacks, both warm and cold.
"Ever tasted dew on a sunny morn?"
"Only once, but I felt reborn!"

With each giggle, dreams take flight,
In this leafy realm of sheer delight.
Vines twine around with laughter's grace,
As they cradle dreams in this happy space.

Beneath the Twisted Boughs

Beneath the twisted boughs, I seek,
A squirrel with secret plans to speak.
He chases his tail, oh what a sight,
In his tiny mind, he wins each fight.

The birds gossip loud, they squawk in fun,
While a bear does yoga, stretching in the sun.
Every leaf whispers a joke or two,
Making nature chuckle; it's all so true.

A bunny prances, hops with flair,
While butterflies giggle, dancing in air.
The mushrooms sit grinning, no care in sight,
Gossiping mushrooms, what a delight!

So let's toast a root beer to this merry band,
To the laughter of nature, isn't it grand?
With each twig's tickle and breeze's cheer,
Life beneath branches is one big jeer.

Nature's Quiet Reverie

In nature's realm, where giggles dwell,
A hedgehog tells riddles; we can't quite tell.
With spines so sharp but jokes so round,
Laughter erupts from the soft ground.

A wise old owl squints, quite confounded,
As raccoons, critters, all gather, astounded.
Each tree seems to chuckle with glee,
As they ponder who sits on the tallest tea.

The frogs strike poses while croaking their song,
In a chorus so funny, you can't help but long.
Their leaps like dance moves, so silly, so bold,
As laughter ripples, every leaf unfolds.

But mind the chipmunk, he's plotting with flair,
A treasure hunt under his leafy lair.
Stealing snacks from a picnic, oh what a sight,
Nature's quiet reverie—joy ignites!

Ponderings of the Wilderness

In the woods where worries cease to hold,
A fox wears glasses; he thinks he's bold.
Contemplating life with a scholarly gaze,
While a raccoon rummages in his crazed ways.

A turtle slowly thinks, while taking a stroll,
Pondering poetry, that's his goal.
The wise old crickets chirp with delight,
Sharing mysteries in the moon's silver light.

Tall grasses sway, laughing at deer,
Who try to be stealthy but trip on a spear.
Every step is a fumble, quite full of grace,
As they blush in the shadows, hiding their face.

So gather, dear friends, for a grand woodland gig,
Amidst all the pondering, we render quite big.
With every chuckle, let your spirit soar,
For wilderness wisdom is never a bore.

Veiled Verses in the Woods

In veiled verses where secrets peek,
The shadows dance, and squirrels speak.
Red ants march past in a parade so grand,
Each carrying crumbs in a tiny hand.

The whispering leaves share stories untold,
About the shades their branches hold.
The raccoons wear masks, quite the disguise,
Stealing lunch under moonlit skies.

A wandering moose plays hide and seek,
Wading through ponds, finding it sleek.
With each splash and snort, what a funny affair,
All creatures join in, with laughter to share.

So tiptoe along where the jests are spun,
In this verdant theater, everyone's won.
For beneath every bough, and behind each breeze,
Are verses of humor amongst the trees.

Reflections in the Briars

In the brambles, creatures dance,
Squirrels twirl, their nuts askance.
A rabbit giggles, hops around,
While thorns poke gently at the ground.

A wise old owl gives a hoot,
"Why don't you guys dance with your boots?"
The hedgehogs laugh, in spiky suits,
While grasshoppers strum their roots.

The breeze whispers secrets of the day,
As dandelions float and sway.
"What's next?" they ponder, with a grin,
A game of hide and seek begins!

But late at night, they tend to snore,
While fireflies light the leafy floor.
In the thickets, laughter's found,
A joyful echo, all around.

Unseen Paths of Reflection

Beneath the leaves, a parade flows,
With ants in hats, they strike a pose.
A spider weaves a disco ball,
Inviting all, come one, come all!

"Oh, watch your step," a worm declares,
As it wriggles through imaginary stairs.
The beetles boast of super speed,
While caterpillars munch a weed.

In sunlit spots, the shadows play,
The grass giggles, "It's a sunny day!"
A fence lizard does a silly dance,
Hoping to catch a lady's glance.

But when the sun sinks low and deep,
The critters gather, secrets to keep.
In this woodland silliness, they dwell,
A world of laughter, where all's well.

Musings of the Mossy Ground

On the mossy carpet, soft and green,
A turtle yawns, "What a sleepy scene!"
A stomp from frogs, a ribbit cheer,
They leap and croak, without a fear.

Next to a log, a party brews,
With mushrooms wearing colorful shoes.
A fox joins in, with a flair and spin,
Creating grooves with a cheeky grin.

The snails in slow-mo snicker and slide,
While a flying squirrel takes a wild ride.
"Hey, what's the rush?" a mockingbird quips,
As it lands near, tending to its scripts.

Their laughter rises with the mist,
In this quirky world, who could resist?
With every giggle, they make their mark,
In the happy woods, where joy embarks.

The Language of Twisted Roots

In the roots and twigs, a chatter's found,
As gophers gossip about the ground.
"Did you see that dance?" a chipmunk sighs,
"Quite the talent, those firefly guys!"

A raccoon cooks up a stick-leaf stew,
While frogs provide the dinner crew.
"Dinner's ready; hop in line!"
Each critter laughs, "This feast is fine!"

A wise old pine joins with a creak,
"Listen closely, hear the trees speak."
The whispers of laughter float in the air,
Even the brambles join in the fair.

As dusk settles in, games disappear,
With twinkling stars, the night draws near.
In the twisted roots, joy takes flight,
A symphony of laughter through the night.

Reflections on Wandering Paths

In tangled lanes where I meander,
A squirrel scolds me, oh how grander!
He chatters loud with nuts in tow,
While I just laugh, and onward go.

The hawk above is clever, spry,
I swear he winked as I passed by.
With every twist, a jest to find,
The jests of nature, oh so kind!

Among the thorns and cheeky snickers,
I lose my way amidst the flickers.
A bush with berries starts to tease,
"Pick us quick, before you freeze!"

So on I stroll, with grin unknotted,
As butterflies march, quite doted.
In woods where laughter freely sings,
The leading mind is not of kings!

Enigmas in Briar and Bramble

Through briars thick, I hear a giggle,
A rabbit hops, and I just wiggle.
His nose is twitching, how absurd,
He seems to plot, why so disturbed?

A carpet of leaves holds secrets bound,
And rustled whispers swirl around.
"Is that a shrub? Or just a joke?"
The shadows dance, they're never broke!

The hedgehog grins, he's full of pranks,
While I am here, giving thanks.
With every step, a riddle sprouts,
What laughs at night? The croaking doubts!

In bramble's clutch, I lose my wits,
As thorny vines play little tricks.
But in this maze, with chuckles bright,
I'd choose it all, and feel just right!

The Heartbeat of Untamed Growth

Among the ferns, a mystery brews,
A squirrel jests, sharing his views.
"Why chase your tail when you can jest?
Join me here, it's for the best!"

The grass ticks me, like a feather,
Each step I take, it pulls together.
"Beware the roots, they're full of quirks,"
It whispers low as mischief lurks!

Beneath the vines, where shadows play,
A gnome peeks out, just to say:
"Have you heard the latest news?
The toadstools wear the finest shoes!"

So let's rejoice, and skip a beat,
In wild growth that brings such heat.
While nature laughs, we'll dance along,
In this big world, where we belong!

Arcana of the Twisted Branches

The branches twist like wacky tales,
Where whispers float on breezy trails.
With knots and turns, the wise old trees,
Conspire to share their funny tease.

A parrot squawks, his jokes are bold,
I swear he's got the secrets told.
"Why wear a hat? Just stick with feathers!"
His caws ring out like playful leathers!

The roots below hold laughter tight,
In every nook, there's pure delight.
A trail of giggles leads me on,
Through leafy lanes till dusk has gone.

Arcane are paths, yet full of fun,
A meandering laugh, under the sun.
With chalky hands and muddy feet,
I leave my worries, oh what a treat!

Impressions of Leafy Sentinels

In quiet shades where shadows play,
Leaves gossip loudly, come what may.
They wave and dance, a leafy spree,
Even the acorns join in glee.

A squirrel pauses, strikes a pose,
With nuts piled high, who really knows?
The branches chuckle, swaying free,
As nature's jesters, wild and spree.

The wind seems to tickle the boughs,
Who knew trees could act so loud?
Their laughter rustles in the air,
An orchestra of jokes laid bare.

So next you stroll through woods so grand,
Stop, listen close, you'll understand.
The sentinels in leafy hats,
Are just as silly as the chats!

The Heartbeat of the Wild

Bees buzz and hum in a crazy whirl,
While grasshoppers dance and twirl.
The deer pull faces, stick out their tongues,
While birds sing anthems that sound like bungs.

Frogs leap, croak, then start to laugh,
As a rabbit trips on a fallen path.
Nature's comedy, a stunning sight,
Where even the snails race with delight.

Mice tell tales of grand escapades,
Trading secrets in the glades.
The bushes giggle, they can't contain,
Amusement in the wild domain.

So hear the rhythm of this place,
Nature's laughter, a happy face.
The heartbeat of wild, loud and clear,
Is filled with joy and a hint of cheer.

Whispers Amongst the Leaves

Leaves flutter soft, with whispers low,
Sharing secrets only they know.
A crow hears rumors, caws with praise,
As sunlight dances in playful ways.

The bushes giggle at the squirrels' flair,
In acorn hats, they prance with care.
A butterfly teases a bumblebee,
'Catch me if you can!' with glee.

Fluffy clouds join the leafy chat,
Hinting at rain like a chitchat spat.
While beetles march, their armor bright,
In nature's comedy, pure delight.

So tune your ears to leafy spots,
For laughter lives in quiet plots.
Amidst the trees, such joy unfurls,
In the murmurs and the swirls!

Secrets in the Underbrush

In the underbrush, a stir and shake,
A hedgehog sneezes, for goodness' sake!
While ants parade with tiny boots,
Marching to rhythm, oh, what hoots!

A lizard grins, all dressed in green,
Strutting his stuff, a real scene queen.
Mice throw parties, cheese on the side,
In tangled roots where they often hide.

The flowers gossip about the skies,
While bees craft plans with wily eyes.
'Join the fun! Let's have a ball!'
'Bring the nectar—let's have a call!'

So in the underbrush, wild and free,
Lies a theater of glee and spree.
Where secrets dance and laughter sings,
In nature's heart, joy truly springs!

Lightning Source LLC
Chambersburg PA
CBHW071846160426
43209CB00003B/438